The Desert Mothers

ALSO BY NATHANIEL TARN

POETRY

Old Savage/Young City (1964) / *Where Babylon Ends* (1969)
The Beautiful Contradictions (1969; 2nd edition 2013)
October (1969) / *The Silence* (1969)
A Nowhere for Vallejo (1971) / *Section: The Artemision* (1973)
The Persephones (1974; revised editions, 2008, 2016)
Lyrics for the Bride of God (1975)
The House of Leaves (1976; 2nd edition 2018*) / *The Microcosm* (1977)
Atitlán / Alashka [Alashka with Janet Rodney] (1979)
Weekends in Mexico (1982) / *The Desert Mothers* (1984; 2nd edition 2018*)
At the Western Gates (1985; 2nd edition 2018*)
Palenque: Selected Poems 1972-1984 (1986*) / *Seeing America First* (1989)
Home One (1990) / *The Army Has Announced that Body Bags…* (1992)
Caja del Río (1993) / *Flying the Body* (1993) / *The Architextures* (2000)
Three Letters from the City: The St. Petersburg Poems (2001)
Selected Poems: 1950-2000 (2002) / *Recollections of Being* (2004)
Avia (2008*) / *Ins & Outs of the Forest Rivers* (2008) / *Gondwana* (2017)
Alashka [with Janet Rodney] (first separate publication, 2018*)

TRANSLATIONS

Pablo Neruda: *The Heights of Macchu Picchu* (1966)
Pablo Neruda: *Selected Poems* (1968) / Victor Segalen: *Stelae* (1969)
Con Cuba (1969) / The Rabinal Achi, Act 4 (1973)
The Penguin Neruda (1975)

PROSE

*Views from the Weaving Mountain:
Selected Essays in Poetics & Anthropology* (1991)
Scandals in the House of Birds: Shamans & Priests on Lake Atitlán (1998)
*The Embattled Lyric:
Essays & Conversations in Poetics & Anthropology* (2007)

* from Shearsman Books

Nathaniel Tarn

The Desert Mothers

Shearsman Library

Second Edition. First U.K. publication.
Published in the United Kingdom in 2018 by
The Shearsman Library
an imprint of Shearsman Books
50 Westons Hill Drive
Emersons Green
BRISTOL
BS16 7DF

Shearsman Books Ltd Registered Office
30–31 St. James Place, Mangotsfield, Bristol BS16 9JB
(this address not for correspondence)

www.shearsman.com

ISBN 978-1-84861-591-5

ACKNOWLEDGEMENTS
Pages 7–38 were first published in chapbook form by
Salt-Works Press, Grenada, MS, 1984, as *The Desert Mothers*.

Weekends in Mexico was originally published
as a chapbook by Oxus Press, London in 1982.

'Dog Viewing Deer' was first collected in *Palenque: Selected Poems 1972-1984*,
jointly published by Oasis Books and Shearsman Books in London, 1986.

The Mothers of Matagalpa was originally published
as a chapbook by Oasis Books, London in 1989.

Contents

Flight from the Mountaintop

In memoriam Edward Dorn

"Aber Freund! wir kommen zu späat. Zwar leben die Götter,
Aber über dem Haupt droben in anderer Welt."
—*Hölderlin*

1

Running off the mountain:
      billow of air,
ground drops below peak,
multicolored sails swerving
        above the valley:
not us flying those wings
      but flown by them.
    (Tangle unraveled:
    the compelling
    drag on the bird... feet and legs in lime,
    beak in his own thick blood,
    needles sticking thru feathers,
      all that behind us.)
Now: arrows, spears, lances,
        columns, towers of air:
      victory headless at the crest,
      yet throat spouting song,
      stump bare and hardly bleeding.

        In their dreams men are
    (gods)
he had said,
    in reflection: SLAVES
Ground is philosophy,
      the hospital –
but the air
      six thousand feet above the valley:
you can't think of wreckage.

In his flight
remembered the isle of light,
        how one morning
had borrowed father's wings,
strapping them on as if for combat, and had
neighbored the sun awhile in soaring lovelike
and free with birds, angels and all manner of
musical spheres, planets and meteors...

In their dreams (he had sd.) men were
        alike.
Dumb bums below, his life was bound up with
        in scalding slavery,
failed to recognize
his cataract out of that morning sky,
        blood like the lightest wine
dissolved in sun and aether.
        He could not have been
salvaged out of that air in any shape
recognizable to man, beast, god,
once he had started falling and
you could not have looked into his eyes
since the sun had taken them quite out.
        But his mind from then on – we are told
in his final speech – what a hoard that was
of incisive tools, and how well he knew
what he wanted around him and what
had to be trashed, like old shoes,
                        outside his door.

"in the dream,
the glide descends in spirals
down to the extremity of my country
from which a ship will take you
                              to the farthest peninsulae
of all other imaginable countries.
It is a winter there
                  I had previously thought
                                          unfathomable."

"In deepest winter
          coldest things calm most.
Causing the mind to desist from raving and to still
inexhaustible choice that is making us all mad.
My gods how I pity you all in this iron age
and want silence now, from now on, always,
and shall not speak to you anymore, nor fly with you,
holding your hands in the sun, protecting your wings,
shielding the delicate wax on your shoulders
from his deadly bite."

"What it had occurred to me to say
concerned the birds of deepest winter in my country,
out of a north larger than memory,
perhaps full of mountains off whose peaks they flew,
which had now congregated for my eyes' pleasure
on the border black lakes of my country:
all that sludge on the lakes like sick thought
sensing its own destruction.
          The end as I had predicted
     (that silent end full of bombardments)
of intellect."

"Is not the metaphor of our indited clarity
that exquisite bird, part white, part black,

whose very head, the pattern of the head,
            is our question mark?
I forget (deliberately)
birds of one color,
even the great
            ghost-trampler of women,
or the black lout of the sea in all his forms,
who stands for the night of the sea in all his forms,
            and has no name, or,
if you will, a multitude, no matter."

"– Your Majesty, my pilots sick today,
unfit for battle. They will not *think*
at the controls, they are dangerous.
I remember the country of the living,
            how they spoke in tongues,
the orders they gave, and the surrenders.
      I was granted today the order of silence.
      Already I don't remember speech.

Speech, I think, was like that very wide
                  river behind my house
very beautiful in the cold air of winter,
                  the blues especially,
carrying the perspective of all human things,
                  whether you looked
back to the source of the river, or down to the sea.
                  It is time
perhaps to move inland and look for walls.
            A tower perhaps.
My wife, held back by her own husband always
      (an air-traffic controller)
might not get around to making it with me.
I don't know whether it will be possible to fly again:
      my flights may be long and impressive,
            but will not be visible anymore.

Je suis hors concours.
These are the elegies, which is: a search for
the origin which does not belong to our deathless order.
And yet we are commanded to purify mankind
and the sentinel number I have posited as
characteristic of the nightly eras of the earth."

3

And let me add
that if it were not for my own extreme sympathy with him:
I mean he who has delivered this poem to you this way,
I could not have spoken like this
nor begun to tell you
that in this America we now have
    a dreampath again, or spirit quest if you will,
departing every day from the mountain top –
                        billow of air underwing
    ground lost below height,
        altho it is not certain that anyone will look
at the finest flyers as they perform in the blue sky,
in the thunderhead sky with tones of copper or iron,
in the misted sky at zero/zero –
        whether they soar beyond the sun
    or collapse into the sea below
        or fix the shape of their outspread arms and legs
on the crumpled ground
                    (slaves to reflection),
    the middle of their bodies pulverized
                    by the effort of flight
and the order of angels closed for the time of this era
                    to any candidate whatsoever.

The Bay Dies of Pollution
& Decoys Rise in Price

for Mark McNair

1

Thinking of her at breakfast
close by Annapolis, between two bouts of talk,
who bears with equanimity
grief's ships, my fleet, over her sea of patience
and that we are as familiar
to each other now as birds
in the great lines of geese yesterday night
while we were crossing Maryland –
when the sky became immense, translucent bowls
nested within each other
and their horizons stretched all the way west
to a distant house where we would soon migrate!
And the numbers of those birds
weaving their leaves of absence in the sky,
the number of those birds in that depth of sky!
Thinking that she haunts me
like an "azure" I have almost forgotten exists
whether it be in the poem
or in the depth of that sky which is reality
and which I still sometimes leave home for
to touch a base or two…

2

The association of beauty and pain
– "beauty is but the beginning of terror
we are unable to bear" – and this morning
on the Bay beyond the storming waters
in a smoke of Fall leaves and comfortable kitchens:
eating: Roman disasters of blue crab
smithereen-smashed on paper tablecloths –
allows some domesticity to dispel the pain.
The Names of the Great Carvers in my mind
and their achievements, like crests and shields,
postered around us – the birds, the "BIRDS",
the lovely, feather-perfect, bobbing birds,
the magnificent art of carving, what it signifies,
the whole Bay culture still breathing in them
as the Bay itself dies of pollution
and decoys rise in price.
I know once more a door shut in my face,
the market suddenly jumping way out of reach
and the carvings swallowed by money,
and for this once, which might be the last time,
I'll go back without a "bird" under my arm:
(trivial misfortune – yet the whole fate of "art"
and its true destination bound in that question),
no: the great ocean beyond the window is not
deep enough to encompass loss
which encompasses little by little all we love –
the bitterness of it, the uncounted days
working at the pile's bottom for pittances,
lifetime of small doors closing.

3

In the radiance – luminism, luminescence –
in the breaking blastoff of American light
returning to haunt me when I least expect it,
blessed gift of the continent I have chosen:
the delicacy of the ships,
the small Bay Bugeyes and Skip Jacks
lying at rest among the fanning swans –
and behind them, the small wooden houses
almost like miniatures in a toy farm.
Going home tonight, carrying nothing
but for a two-bit flag "Don't Give Up The Ship",
empty-handed it seems, not yet recalling the words,
the treasury of words opening up
when least expected,
appearing out of nowhere like long lines of geese.

The White Widow

in memoriam Kenneth Rexroth

1

On returning from *Les Contes d'Hoffman,* modern version – *Tootsie* – first sight ever of the illustrious small death raveling her nest a span away from the foot of the desk.

Worshipfully elegant she is indeed, jet black, a stop sign on her belly keeping the watch tonight.

Mild movement of the legs as if caught like algae in a tropical stream.

The light turned on, vanishes timidly down one of the innumerable sutures of the house.

Night slithers from the bottom of a coffin. Someone massaging us lifts her hands to our throats and produces the strangled howl known locally as the "cry from the dead".

After which the stop sign flashes at regular intervals, all night, for seven hours.

One man recognizes our language. He answers. Life can continue for one more day.

The torrent of his conversation nearby, as if the dry river bed had suddenly filled with snows distilled from the bluest bloods of the sky.

2

White banner of the samoyed, waving as if under-water, dallying past the four king spaniels of lot one (plus the horse and the burro); the two jack bloodhounds of lot two and the graying queen shepherd of lot three, growling and rushing her.

Following on the black long dog from the south, whose ass had put an end to all philosophies when seen processionally for a certain time.

The white princess waves and flirts, backs and crouches, noses around, bounds for the final rush at a speed exceeding light's. Doe eyes. Ruff of smiles.

While the illustrious lady in the black cart has not appeared this morning. She still breathes and breeds under the study floor.

And the debate as to what to do with her kind continues around the communal table: can we possibly cohabit?

3

Dream of cohabitation like the smile on a favorite face among the thousand caves where we had left incense burning for you at your news. Land where death's flag is reversible.

Though you might have preferred the streams of Tulufan, musical among willows, or the misted lake below the cataract of the Summer Palace, or the pool under monastery walls, climbing Emei.

Dream of all anger turning to fear, then fear one day dropping like the wind, leaving the sun of justice to shine in the western sky.

Hold up our hands to the light. The small black personage dances on our palms with her elegant legs lifting her above our lines of fate. She grows transparent and, while your voice chances on, becomes almost invisible. Then she is visible again, bone white, in the relentless desert air that leaves no room for anything but clarity.

El Rancho, Condado de Santa Fe, 1.83.

The Desert Mothers

Entering into This

for J.R., in no way differently.

Granted that
      life is
  irremediably *dukkha:*
       dis-comfort, dis-satisfaction,
Dis, in this life above ground
   which is mostly shadow, in which light
must be introduced, dab at a time:
   fingertip, brush of eyelid, chest hair,
aura round the generation machine in its upstanding
      jus/tice – and finally that light
so hard won is shaded, stroke by stroke, by the same
   pencil in its pride of darkness,
drawing you down to Dis in this life…
       Whoever promised
all floors were different: "in my mansion, many rooms"
but did anyone say, this room, that, will be a garden?
Did anyone promise? Did one say tulips? roses? maple
just before snow: the ultimate in fire? Or ever say
snow – whose white defeats those strokes for blind days?
     Then, if you, yes, I thought if you would, grant
such a premise, we could rest from hope in the definite,
    you and I – this hope knowledge would be ours
WHOLE – after the escalation. And no more climb. The
mountains are, last enough if last is any point to make,
while the world's flowers take our eyes on down
  to the canyons arush with crazy April waters –
   Where we see the great wall move at us, take us,
and we wait for it, standing stock still.

Or That the President Would Abdicate

They never dreamed it.
　　　Or that the president,
discussing his wars with a general,
　　　should give one thought to a soldier,
a common man, or
　　　initiate consideration of his fate
　　　　　and, by extension,
perhaps call off the war: no,
　　　no president will talk, except of other leaders,
　　　　　as if to say: kings? KINGS? *what* kings?
Thrones are well-oiled, kings always protected.
　　　Now think, not even *of* the soldier,
　　　　　think THE soldier, the SOLDIER:
how his life beds down in the dust
　　　and he has not been asked.
That there are, oh, untold millions of soldiers,
　　　and they have not been asked.
And now, you can bring out the poems,
　　　the autumn poems especially,
color of blood – and you can swear that this time
　　　the poems will be difficult.
　　　　　　　Not to excavate,
but to bring forth:
　　　they need to be torn from their hinges.
You have been putting off this moment
　　　for most of your existence now,
　　　　　(that use of *now*) and NOW,
it is inescapable: the poem's new
　　　　　or else, each time, a soldier dies for it.
　　　　　　Or that the president would die,
walk off into a grove, to be blinded there,
step up to a hill, to be hung from a cloud,
　　　slide into a gully, to be mangled by animals –
but go, GO, it would be time for him to GO.

Silence approaches,
a lonesome, ancient man.
         All are gone home. You are the poet.
With silence moving towards you,
         and you trying to work your throat, your voice,
                  the ice-blue mind.

For the Rules of Flight

Like a plane
        caught in the slipstream
                of another, and unable,
for the rules of flight,
        to drop or soar, out of the stream,
                so here and now,
so here and now I cannot
drop off this path taking me down into pain,
        as my feet, constrained,
                walk me into pain, as my arms,
swing me towards it,
        as my face greets, as my mouth,
                opens and states the message
that will infuriate the crowd, saying, look:
        I do not know the way to go,
                I only know, this way, this way
you go
        is not the one it should be.
                Then a bird,
multi-colored, magnificent, eyeing us with knowledge
        of what should be done,
free from the rules of flight as the plane is not,
        appears to save the day for all of us:
                until you say:
Ah, everyone is waiting to be saved –
and for how many, for how many can this be done?
                        We had hoped today
the weather might do what it has done for weeks now, smile:
        because today we go out to look at our house,
                the house of the remainder of our lives.
                        And for once,
in all these months, it snows.
        The sky is dark,
                the horizon out.

Views are invisible.
And over the invisible mountains, the flights continue,
    planes and birds,
        constrained or free.
Architects, awaiting clearance, eye the sky's angles.

Death Fear — Yet of Another

It is not a fear —
  though he is going out of his mind,
    though his words
tumble over each other so fast,
  no idea can ever form completely,
    and the drift, the drift is only
towards the dead and exhaustion of meaning.
It is not a fear,
  because there is no thing
    that you can name to fear:
it is a trepidation, a war in the nerves,
  electric wires on fire in the brain,
    reaching to the idea,
but never getting where
  you can say: ah, there it is,
    clear, shining, the star
towards which I have always traveled,
  whose light I've seen
even though it began before my birth.
  He is MAD. It is difficult to say he is *mad*
  for to define true madness
  is no true rest.
But that
  not getting at
    no thing that we can
name, can hold, can change
  into the star, or image of the star,
even remembrance, symbol,
  any remotest memoration of that star:
            this is the terror, building
temples, observatories,
  as if the architecture tried to lift itself
and HE, still babbling,
  from somewhere back of where we are,

way back to ARCHE, of which the LOGOS, lost,
sustains and feeds the trepidation.
As if something like cancer
were going to be announced,
and all of life dissolve,
as the crab once took my love into the sea,
under the deepest rock to lie,
as one lies on one's back
to be boned.
Do not worry, the friend says:
he is not among the living,
this babbler.
Those people I worked with, they would say:
he is gone among the *Bao* (i.e, the dead).
Which he already speaks with,
is loved by, with love we cannot know.

Animal Bride

The desire to write
    sits by the thigh
        of a god emerging from the dead,
come from a house in the fist of an iron mountain,
    blue above the bluest of air.
We hear the god's heart and the drum moving it
    into the four directions.
This week, there were too many people
    intersecting lives and conversations.
        The information came too thick at us,
slow poison in a noxious cloud.
    It is exciting, this information –
        that's not the point –
but the corn meal, flying about in clouds,
    settles into no cup.
        And to make it move, this world,
the cup needs to be full,
    brimming and still.
            The house
in the iron fist is still
    because it's in a postcard above the desk,
a window into the infinite of our wills:
    here, the Mummy Cave,
    here, the Potala,
    here, the Summer Palace,
plunging to the lake
    with a cloud of blossom enveloping
the god's dream of you and I on this earth
    in our daily wars.
No man, no woman is a place
    to be arrived at, to be departed from.
        No animal dreams the dead as destination
to rise in the world, to grant a sustenance.
            Give me back my heart!

And then, if the animal,
        the soul-struck being,
dreaming her pelt covered with feathers,
        as if to fly up, up,
to her place where she alone is sovereign,
        and no master calls her back
                to sup or sleep at the dismal time.
But the master has no soul,
        abandons the animal,
                the sweetsmiling, doe-eyed
        bare-toothed animal in love,
                leaves her at the corner of a road,
                        by the thigh of the god
where she emerged in the first place,
        deaf to all conversations,
                wanting only to come to him, to wed him.

Peredur West

Smell of the desert
before the sun eliminates all shadows:
the rider who would write us down
as if we had not lived
    breathes it in completely
        entering the canyon
his lungs awash with childhood perfumes.
    Westwards he moves, his right hand held
    by the invisible daughter of the earth.
Motherwards he moves, back to his homeland,
the lady leading him has promised it:
    he grants her trust implicitly.
    Recites the names of the first landowners
    bringing a map to life that had been lost
    since the disaster he alone survived.
        She leads him to a fountain
in the canyon's heart
    which they had tried to quench in the old days
but the fountain sang a wound
    and never could be quenched.
        Star of the Desert, he begins to sing,
        Rose of Sand,
        here I stand at my father's fountain
        and you have left it utterly,
        waters that once sang joyously
        drowning the reason for all tears
        have turned to sand and bones are now
        all my solace day or night.
It is here he begins to write us down,
    here he takes off his leathers
and is dressed in armor like the sun.
Facing the mesas jagged like a saw
    with teeth fit for a giant's grinding jaw,
        he now moves further west.

Even so, travel helps the weary poet
    moving a song back to his heart.
Brighter than a thousand suns,
    his father shines against his breastplate,
strikes from his lance
    a thousand shards of light.
        His eyes are put out now,
he writes by touch,
    guiding the quill with his free hand.
Blind I return to my father's land,
    blind, I accept my mother's curdled milk,
blind, I shall write us down with our last ashes.
Poverty, he says, as he enters the mesas,
naming them for the gift he has gotten of God.

Rainer Werner Moves His Lady
from Hollywood to Heaven

in memoriam R. W. Fassbinder

Driving through night,
up from the south:
there goes a car leaning towards Colorado!
   We have come up from The Angles and The Crosses,
looking for birds in the Gila,
        the April migration north
and we remember,
    from as far south as the Land of Fire they call it –
          which may be Hades
that he has gone now.
   Telling us. He has told us,
     laid out in front of us, in all its detail,
       the image of his going.
He has explained it about as close as it is possible to do
without explicitly…: o.k., here, in so and so many days,
this is what I shall do, and how I'll do it.
                      He was looking
for a flatter tone,
trying to get away from that voice for which he had
been known, towards some other people would only hear
                  when he was gone.
In each story,
   he brought a different character forward,
      making that character the lead – and the others,
who had been the lead in his other stories,
      were quite content to play minor parts
   shining like small birds,
moving north in the spring of April when the birds
    start that strange, annual movement,
      never a year seeming different from another.
   We are touching a place
   where there are no changes,

where the bells do not ring changes
    or a different music,
but the song of he who stays put,
    who turns
        throughout the night to stone.
I think people will see in time,
  like they see us coming north from the south,
    that he was moving in a direction
no one had ever shown from the south,
  to an untenable north his actress would kill,
so putting an end to the story.
                            And notice:
    this is the final story, (or
    we think it is, we don't yet know,)
the last telling, NOTICE:
    that the lady is hearing a new song
    from the birds moving up in April:
    it is a song of FREIHEIT, FREEDOM,
      of the REPUBLIC of Friedrich,
    (except that Rainer Werner always calls him Franz,
    Franz being the contemporary incarnation
    of our guardian, Magister Friedrich.)
    And what the new song is, against all likelihood,
    is a song showing, in the ground of suffering,
    impossible incarceration, from which no liberty
    can ever free a single Rainer Werner
    and/nor a singling trembling biped in his chains:
(with memory, say, of Treblinka, Dachau, Auschwitz,
Terezín's violins chiming with April birds
  as we drive north in the night
    and a car leans towards Colorado!)
Wyomings are unthinkable.
  Montanas still more so.
    Canadas: why they are nearly at the ice!
                    He must move west
                    where the sun dies
                    on the outskirts of Hollywood.

Then, if he moves the lady from Hollywood to Heaven,
    he ends the story.
The President of France cannot;
    The Führer of Germany; the Duce of Italy;
        all dukes, counts, marquesses: they cannot save it.
The English Emperor;
    The Indian Viceroys; the Mandarins;
        the great-grand children of the Khans cannot save it:
the story cannot be saved.
    A silver mirror shows us the grand finale of Europe,
brought on by one lone African out of the south,
                the land of Fire.

In one story, he was a lover, almost a god.
But for a long time now, he has played bit parts
                and, for all his size,
he is as puny as a warbler flying up from Fire,
                flaming through the Gila,
    to where he may winter and nest. And even breed.
        There is no breeding in Rainer Werner.
His is a short-cut through the back mirror of a man,
    there is no fleshing there:
    nothing to program bones and muscles
        that will structure a future.
            The future does not play on our knees.
For lack of a future, Rainer Werner says goodbye
to the grand opera howling as winds sweep through trees,
setting fire to all Brazil on our way north and out.
    She is dead: the lady of the future.
    We sit in the dark, waiting to hear her dream.
        She stares out of Hades, which is down south,
    mouthing something about freedom.
        She is caught. She has sold her present.
    Sold her future. Has nothing left but her death
            to offer to the story.
In a panic, mouth wide open, howling down a storm
we do not see but know is going on behind the panes,

as the sun streams out of her room on an Easter morning,
    in that panic she swallows
        her death and the story.

We move north.
   It is a fearsome trepidation keeping the voice flat
   in spite of our sense of the end
   that has come to the story.
Driving back through the night
(because we have made it to the north and come back
and move north again, for the nth time, through the April)
   – but no one knows this –
on its long slow journey, in desperation,
its tires losing air as they go,
the car we follow leans out towards Colorado –
                  and we make it home:
   to move again the next day
    towards THE CROSSES AND THE ANGLES
              on which Rainer Werner's story
is HUNG.

Weekends in Mexico

A Departure

Waking to music
in Pennsylvania
dawn chorus
first orchestrations,
wander around the house
thinking of food and wash
later the workliness,
break open curtains
on the greening garden,
turn from routine
to clamber down
all the deep stairs
to the front door
open where no one knocks
wide to the air
open the door
walk into Mexico

El Tepozteco

This fold
the earth makes
just here
throwing up mountains
like gigantic
Chinese gardens
this light
at this window
these leaves
parting the sky
this patch
of violent color
bougainvillea
roses
this fire inside
all the places
we should by rights
be living in
united here
in this bright
stillness
these limbs at rest
stilled heart
stilled mind
but busy hands
fingering the light

Origin of the Order of
Sto. Domingo de Guzman, Oaxaca

Heads in hand
at the level of morning,
rising at dawn
heads in hand,
presenting beads
at the convent gate
from the four corners
at the level of morning,
unable to leave
the convent precincts
unable to find
another home –
this is the lineage
dead in the night
by unknown hands
going back inside
to save itself,
at the level of morning
at the tree's base
where the roots suffer
climbing the ladder
to spreading branches
from the four corners
to the four ribs closing
on heaven's lock –
the head above
the single center
the eye of light

Querétaro

On the great stage
Querétaro
the prompter's box
whispers old streets
of golden Spain
corner fountains
smelling of piss
wide squares
like ship decks
crystal perspectives
lovers exhibiting
roses instead of teeth
gold altars in their mouths
and senior citizens
hunchbacked
with pockets full of opals.
Baroque retablos soar
from inside the heart
into old skies
weary of religion
hell-soup swilling around
their marble feet.
Like at Santa Rosa
under a rain of gold:
headquarters of
artificial insemination
for todo México –
do they use condoms
in Querétaro
or merely block urethras
with minute opals?

San Xavier, Tepozotlán

Granted grace
that they might fall
from highest peak
touching the sky
peak all of gold:
open windows
wings of embodied
angels with hands
and feet of gold
rain falling
from their feet
all of gold
their hands
all of gold
their golden crotches
fecundating roots
leaves   flowers
fruit   lianas
whole fields
of maize and beans
farms   animals
our earthly life
finally us men
whose gold is inside
with flesh so hard
from work done
on this floor below
it has turned to stone

The Rose from Ajusco

Brought down in her childhood
by a girl meaning well
by our hunger for flowers
reached us as large
and perfect bud
larger than life
usually is for roses
came as a sign
down from the mountains
as if the sky
had broken blood with us
leaving this sum of life with us
all life for a mere week.
And while we traveled
to the golden churches
and silver temples
the rose led her life
in a glass by the bed
not so much flowering
blowing or even dying
in the end, but sharing love
with us. She grew
encompassing the house
swallowing furniture
books   pictures   letters
all messages and calls
remembrances we got
from live and dying friends.
Was deepest crimson
passing into purple
and at the end
abyssal black.
I had never seen a rose
not die as this did not

having at last to be taken down
below the yard and buried
into the weather.
At middle life
she shone and didn't
in various petals varyingly
opening depths
no ordinary flower
had ever plumbed.
She put an end
almost to language
we could not talk about her
but only marvel on
her sounds in us.
The rose as a matter of fact
was a gift from a girl
with strong feelings
hard to express
in all the chatter round us,
her silence spoke
loudest and most enduringly
of huge volcanoes
we saw only once
on our last evening
when the haze lifted once
over above Ajusco
and we were about to leave
and fly for home next morning

Union Mexicana de Organilleros

This morning
in Tepoztlán Mexico
far from home
for the third month running
I think of
our laughing smiling
house and how
good it would be
to be there
a month
or several more
just be there
doing nothing special

Dog Viewing Deer:
Songs of Death, Resurrection
and the Movie Market

First Animal Song

Engaged by destiny
to be born a dog on earth
while the deer
in a whirlwind of flowers
from the heart of his mouth
hurls back the tide of death
out of the planet's plaza
to save all other deer.
The small dog with a broken leg
held out in front of him like a branch
follows the procession
and the lame large dogs
follow the procession,
all saving their souls as best they can
in the shadows of their beaten masters.

First Jesus-the-Sun Song

Are you a friend of Jesus-the-Sun
who married the moon, who married the moon?
— I was his friend when the world was young
and he was climbing a ladder in the sky.
— And are you still a friend of Jesus-the-Sun?
— Now he continues climbing to the sky
but the ladder has long now fallen away,
the ladder has long since fallen away
and it is hard to be friends with such a man.

Second Animal Song

Listen says the little dog:
you can hear the sound
of my heart breaking into flower
as I watch the deer in his storm of drums
dancing in the grove of young greens
while an indigo night hangs above us.
Above this deer flies the deer of the immense sky
holding up the stars cradled on his horns
like angels in arms. I think
says the little dog
there must be a dog of the immense sky
beside him, perhaps holding the moon
in his friendly mouth –
and he licks her with frenzy,
giving her such pleasure
she lolls sideways, her breasts flowing,
as her bed floats up into the sky.

Second Jesus-the-Sun Song

Jesus-the-Sun is a small, lean man
with a scarlet apoplectic face
who never takes any exercise.
He is bald with a crown of snowy hair,
he has a pinched nose and pinball eyes,
an icicle beard drips from his chin.
He tries new words as if his mouth were full of flowers
but they turn to dust on his teeth, falling away
down to the desert floor. His words are gray:
they are the words he's stolen all his life
from the previous Suns. There must be a big bird
invisible to us, eating out of his guts
sometime between the morning star and dawn
at the time it is hardest for us to continue
doing all we've done for life, for several lives.

Third Animal Song

I have cancer says the little dog.
The deer is silent.
It is incurable says the little dog
while the other dogs moan roundabout.
The deer continues silent. After a while:
I am your closest friend says the deer.
– I thought you were the friend of Jesus-the-Sun
who married Mary-the-Moon
says the little dog while the other dogs weep.
The deer's eyes fill with tears descending
from where they have been cradled on the horns.
It is all one says the deer. The little dog nods.
But he thinks that Jesus has never had cancer.
It is a private thought he keeps to himself
as he joins yet another procession around town.

Fourth Animal Song

Unmistakable glamor attaches to the deer.
His profile is finer than Rudolf Valentino's
and his chest is a symposium of movie stars.
His headcloth disappears into another life,
the life of Hollywood perhaps or Beverly Hills,
from which the white light of all our joy emerges.
His belt is a sphere of everlasting music,
a belt of maracas and whistling harps,
playing like planets round the sun unceasingly.
His skirt is as dark as swimming pools at night
fringed with the palm trees of desert America,
holding Mary-the-Moon locked into his thighs
like Dorothy Lamour in a slipstream of fishes.
His ankles rasp their bones when rubbed together
so that the dead talk together, passing messages.
His feet reach down into the graves of his sires
back to the first deer buried on mountain tops,
looking down on all the fields and forests they browsed
before man came to Wyoming or to California.
The dog has no ancestors – or they are forgotten,
left behind with Bogie in desert Casablanca,
gone where all the dogs have gone to nothingness.
Dog bones are shattered whistles, dog skins exploded drums.

Coda

To be crucified
is not to be nailed to a tree.
It is to be watched by your closest friends,
the desert deer of the tiptop sky,
while you grow into your own tree –
and they do not take the time off
to unlock their horns
even to pull you down.
Son of Man:
set a dog down
in the middle of anywhere
in this interminable movie
and he will start about his business
immediately sniffing
despite the fact that it is ANYWHERE.
For us. And what is anywhere
to a dog? And what is anywhere to us?
How do we know where is WHERE?
and whether to start here, continue, or finish
anything –
        HERE, or in any other space?

The Mothers of Matagalpa

In memoriam Pablo Neruda

les blanches nations en joie
—Rimbaud

Like the freedom of madmen and the insane:
so that there be no thing on earth or elsewhere
                              cannot be said (by us)
insofar exactly as it won't be listened to exactly –
    a deafness
beyond the proverb CAST NOT PEARLS BEFORE SWINE,
                              & easier for a camel through
        the needle's eye
THAN FOR A DEAF MAN TO ENTERTAIN HEAVEN. So go to:

them, entering long hall, sitting down quietly,
face to face with us, sitting down quietly,
        the long sea flowing in the midst,
now speak most simply, enunciating:
        name, age,
        manner of death,
        place of death,
                    relation-ship in love
        down the middle sea,
                    where death began.

SO THAT simple speech versing into song through,
choral simplicity of it, lacking all decoration.
Leader suggesting, suggesting no more, approach:
all ye closer one to another – ye seeking peace.
Them, as to cue, getting up, smoothing eyes, up.
                              appro-
        aching us.

Us, dropping all our sophistication behind us
  on the seat we leave, (approaching us:)
  this difficult, timid, meandering melt
  of middle earth, still human in dimension – then

us, over-tall, -fat, -stocky, children of
  our colossal empire, much more great than death,
  owning it all, giving it down to neighbors,
  all sundry people, over all earth, starting to
stray to stars now presently, taking death also.

  As if: there were *madres sin hijos,*
  (they are mothers without sons),
como si, there were children without mothers,
               each looking for the other,
from a long time before, aching,

emotion beginning to rise, unfamiliar to us minds,
somewhat filling the throat as if we had swallowed another
body than ours and it were falling down our throats, to the
lungs, belly, gut, womb-filling, placental, coming out in
blood between legs as we struggle to: mingle to:
      and the soul
      swimming alone too naked the vast sea.
                 seen gone over ice alone – north
                     further north,
     than anyone outside the empire can imagine.

Madres
not of "heroes and martyrs" like they say
  but simply children, sons, dragged up through years
into some sort of manhood, early here, singing,
               lyric, rhetoric, analytical,

just with the chords of the voice
                    like the one (a month gone by,
        flowers purchased just this morning on the way down here)
            having taken the left eye out,
            cutting the jugular to let the blood free,
            barking that will let the communism out of you,
taking out the back brain – gray spill, gray floor,
turning to mud blood (brown here, out of earth)
(not forgetting the ritual castration), (not) (anything)
(forgetting) to (drain) the mother (sea)

HOW IS IT THAT YOUR PRE-ZI-DENT, with so many teeth,
on his gigantic throne, in all that north,
fears us so much a pimple on the map, so much IN-VI-SI-BLE?
How can he, but for insanity, snakes in the mind,
versing the mind to it, changing maybe the composition of
the very d.n.a. of under-standing?   GO NOW: Act! Act!
                TELL IT LIKE IT IS:
insofar exactly as it won't be listened to exactly –
    deafness to those who think they own
                    the UNI-*VERSE*, the HEMI-*SPHERE*,
the LAND-*GAUGE*: song sung by mother so much long ago, so go,
how could we not but know [CERTAINTY, STILL WITHIN
                                WARRANTY,
NO QUESTIONS ASKED] the way it is, for us, so *there* for them –
in one linguistic god, one lyric, even this structured dog
                between one mother's legs, latent,
that brine of pain, feels empire on his eyes, closes, dozes,
            intelligence asleep to cut from this.

And then the question arises,
as it does among some women, fallen to spasms in one corner,
the whole PACIFIC of it, washed over them again,
    "how do we *do* this? how *can* we do this!"
    – which, upon questioning, reveals

that this is done twice or thrice *a week*

         in "slack times"
but twice or thrice *a day*

      when times are "busy" –
 the country near-dead now of delegationitis –
examined right down to the asshole time over time, to
check if this, permissible, that, permissible, so we can be
COMFORTABLE with this/that, on our high throne up north,
while the buck goes down, going on down, so we can be
COMFORTABLE at this level, low-intensity level, invisibility war…

         So that this dance,
and song, is *not* spontaneous, *not* fit to make the heart
leap up into the mouth for song, as the con-vention goes,
as in-spiration falls, but, while it looks that way, dis-
tances you (Bertolt B.), epic, stopping you, tracks, anal-
ysing you, breaths, repro-ducing you (Walter B.), inform-
acting you (coming to the margin), makes it worth your while,
(coming to the point of sitting this one out) falls to fight
another day, onwordily however:
 as a critique of the discourse of power,
 muriéndome un lunes, un martes, un miércoles qualquiera,
 (sintiéndome un poco lunes al empezar)
      aber Freund! wir kommen zu spät!
  without alternative
      to recover the meaning of words!

but, at least, that we do not fight among ourselves,
using up all that precious energy (*zu spät*)
there being out there all that LABOR,
 m'en allant défendre MA révolution(g)
      in all these souths of the free ocean:

Two hours north+ or – exactly, into the war zone,
but with mothers all over the place, in every city,
village, co-op, who should forbid their thighs perhaps,
as the old poet had it:
                    until they die of.

            AQUÍ NO ONE SURRENDERS.
            NO ONE SURRENDERS HERE.
            AQUÍ NO SE RINDE NADIE.
                                until we die of. And we do.
                                And we do:

It being better to be a fluke in the gut of a sheep
than a poet drowned by chance in the ocean of this *imperium*
      that called itself, once proudly, a REPUBLIC
                        (hail perishing)
                        "and was to be the smile of all the world":

TRASHED, WASTED, DAMN NEAR GONE
                                in mind-rot. Imbecility. Inertia
            of the soul
            swimming alone too naked the vast sea
            asking what will become of us – who should have been

[and the story will be told (later) how, left *or* right,
we require the *land*, and will kill *all* to get it,]

such friends, kissing those mothers' cheeks – fall into action,

as if – meaning the real of it.

A Note from the Publisher

This volume is part of a series that is devoted to recovering out-of-print volumes that – in my view – should be made available again. The books date from the 1970s to the 2000s and all of the first dozen volumes have been important to me in one way or another. Most are long out of print, although some can be found within subsequent collected editions.

The Desert Mothers was a chapbook, first published in an edition of 400 copies in 1994, letterpress-printed and hand-sewn, by the Salt-Works Press of Grenada, Mississippi. The opening poem, 'Flight from the Mountaintop' first appeared in the magazine *Imprint*, which I co-edited, back in 1979.

    The current volume makes no pretence at equalling the high production quality of the Salt-Works edition, but the collection more than earns its place in this Shearsman Library series, because it is now accompanied by some other fine poems of the same period: *Weekends in Mexico* was first published as a chapbook in London by John Stathatos' small press, Oxus Press; *The Mothers of Matagalpa* was first published in London as a chapbook by Ian Robinson's Oasis Press; 'Dog Viewing Deer' was published in the Shearsman Books / Oasis Books joint publication, *Palenque — Selected Poems 1971-1984*, in 1985, having previously appeared in a magazine in the USA. There is thus an unexpected British element in the background of this expanded edition of *The Desert Mothers*…

Tony Frazer
June 2018

www.ingramcontent.com/pod-product-compliance
Lightning Source LLC
Chambersburg PA
CBHW020218090426
42734CB00008B/1123